THE EXTRAORDINARY LIFE OF

ANNE
FRANK

First American Edition 2020
Kane Miller, A Division of EDC Publishing

Original edition first published by Penguin Books Ltd, London
Text copyright © Kate Scott 2019
Illustrations copyright © Anke Rega 2019
The author and the illustrator have asserted their moral rights.

For information contact:
Kane Miller, A Division of EDC Publishing
P.O. Box 470663
Tulsa, OK 74147-0663
www.kanemiller.com
www.edcpub.com
www.usbornebooksandmore.com

Library of Congress Control Number: 2019941859

Printed and bound in the United States of America
1 2 3 4 5 6 7 8 9 10
ISBN: 978-1-68464-072-0

THE EXTRAORDINARY LIFE OF
ANNE
FRANK

Written by Kate Scott
Illustrated by Anke Rega

Kane Miller
A DIVISION OF EDC PUBLISHING

Amsterdam

NETHERLANDS

North Sea

Leeuwarden Groningen

Assen

Amsterdam   Lelystad   Zwolle

Apeldoorn

The Hague   Utrecht   Arnhem

Rotterdam

's-Hertogenbosch   Sonniuswijk

Eindhoven

BELGIUM   GERMANY

WHO WAS
Anne Frank?

Anne Frank

was an ordinary girl with an extraordinary talent,
who faced the hardships of her short life
with courage and good humor.

As a young girl during the Second World War she had to go into **hiding** from the Nazis, who wanted to kill Jews like her. Anne managed to hide in a *secret annex* for over two years. Throughout this time Anne *kept a diary* of everything that happened. It was this diary that would make her famous and become one of the most read and respected books of the twentieth century.

Anne died when she was only fifteen years old, but her name and face have become well-known around the world because of her extraordinary writing.

Anne and her family went into hiding three years after the Second World War began. Only a few people *knew their secret*. Their helpers brought them *food*, risking their own lives for more than two years to help the people in hiding.

But on August 4, 1944, Anne and the others were discovered, *arrested* and taken away. Someone had betrayed their secret.

Of the eight people who had gone into hiding, only Anne's father, **Otto Frank**, survived.

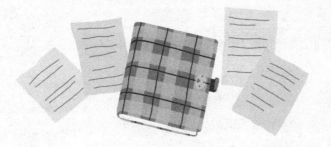

When he discovered Anne's diary he was *amazed* by her words. He showed parts of it to family and friends and they quickly *convinced* him that Anne's diary was special and should be *published*.

Otto Frank devoted the rest of his life to making sure that as many people as possible could read the record of the war that his daughter had created. Otto Frank lived to see her *become famous* around the world.

The diary showed what it was like for Jewish people living through the Second World War. But it also showed how brave, funny and thoughtful Anne was.

She had an outgoing personality and was known to be a "chatterbox," but she showed another side of herself in her diary.

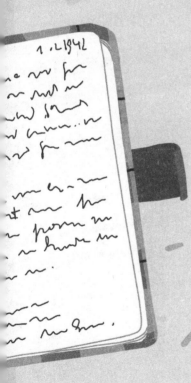

She treated it like a friend and confided all her **deepest thoughts** to it.

Anne's diary is an important *historical document*. It gives us a picture of day-to-day life at a time when food shortages, robberies and cruelty to Jewish people were daily events. In some ways Anne was a *typical teenager*. But she was also capable of *wise words* and entertaining storytelling.

Many years after her death, Anne seems to *leap from the pages* of her diary as someone vibrant and glowing – someone you would like to know.

Let's find out more about Anne and her extraordinary life.

Anne's beginnings

*A*nne was born on June 12, 1929, in Frankfurt am Main, *Germany*. She had an older sister called *Margot*. The Franks were Jewish, and their family had lived in Frankfurt for many generations.

In 1933, when Anne was three years old, Adolf Hitler came to power in Germany. Life for Jewish people changed quickly after this. Just over a month after taking **control of the government**, Hitler told non-Jewish people not to use Jewish businesses. Other anti-Jewish rules and actions followed.

The Nazis and the Jewish People

The Nazis (Adolf Hitler's followers) thought that Jewish people were of less value than Germans. The situation for Jewish people became increasingly dangerous as Hitler gained more power.

By the end of the war millions of Jewish people had been captured and killed, both in Germany and in the countries Hitler's army had invaded and OCCUPIED.

NAZI: "National Socialist German Workers' Party," the political party led by Adolf Hitler.

OCCUPIED: an occupied country is one that has been taken over and is controlled by another country.

Anne Frank's family realized they could be in danger and decided to move to Amsterdam in the Netherlands.

Amster

NETHE

 Brusse

BELGIUM

FRANCE

LANDS

GERMANY

● Cologne

LUXEMBOURG

Frankfurt
●

Mannheim

17

A world at war

Six years later, on September 1, 1939, the Nazi army INVADED Poland. Great Britain declared war on September 3. The two sides were known as the Allies and the Axis powers.

INVADE: to take over another country by force.

The Second World War involved countries from all over the world. The Allies included Great Britain, France, the United States of America and the Soviet Union. The Axis countries included Germany, Italy and Japan. By the end of the war many more countries were fighting for the Allies than for the Axis powers.

The Second World War **LASTED FOR SIX YEARS.** It began on **SEPTEMBER 1, 1939,** and ended on **MAY 8, 1945,** when Germany surrendered.

Six million Jews were murdered during the war – a GENOCIDE known as the *Holocaust.*

GENOCIDE: the intentional act of destroying a whole national, racial, political or cultural group.

Life in Amsterdam

Anne's family had all moved to the Netherlands by early 1934. For the first few years things went well and they were able to lead a normal life. Anne's father set up his own **business** while Edith (Anne and Margot's mother) looked after the **home**. Margot and Anne went to the local school and the two sisters **made friends** there.

Did you know?
Anne Frank had a cat called Moortje who used to greet her by rubbing against her legs.

They began to learn how to speak and write in *Dutch* instead of German. Anne was only four when her family moved to the Netherlands, so she learned the new language very quickly.

Anne and her friends liked to play table tennis. After they had played, they would cycle to an ice cream parlor. Playing table tennis made them hot and ice cream was the perfect answer!

DID YOU KNOW?

Anne formed a table tennis club with four other girls. They called themselves "The Little Dipper Minus Two."

On her thirteenth birthday Anne received several presents. Her gifts included flowers, a blouse, a book and book tokens – as well as a diary.

In her first entry, she calls the diary "one of my nicest presents." What Anne didn't know was that it was to become one of the most important books of the twentieth century!

The first pages of Anne's diary describe her life in Amsterdam and all her friends. Anne decided to treat her diary **like a friend**. Soon after starting to write in it, she even gave her diary a name – *Kitty*. From then on Anne began every entry with "Dearest Kitty."

DID YOU KNOW?

Anne took the name "Kitty" from some books she loved by an author called Cissy van Marxveldt.
Kitty was a friend of the main character of the books, Joop.

"I hope I will be able TO CONFIDE EVERYTHING TO YOU, as I have NEVER been able to confide in anyone, AND I HOPE YOU WILL be a source of COMFORT and support."

When Anne began her diary she wrote *descriptions* of all her friends. Some friends she admired very much, and some she didn't like at all!

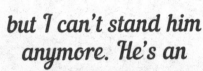

"Rob Cohen used to be **IN LOVE WITH ME TOO,** *but I can't stand him anymore. He's an*

OBNOXIOUS, *two-faced, lying,*

SNIVELING LITTLE TWIT *with an awfully high opinion of himself."*

Because her diary was *private,* Anne could write down exactly what she thought and not worry about being polite!

Anne's parents had hoped that moving to the Netherlands would **keep them safe** from Hitler and the Nazis. But in 1940 Hitler's army **invaded** the country. Shortly afterward the Dutch army surrendered and the Germans took control.

Anne's parents tried to arrange to *leave the country* and move to the United States, but conditions for Jewish people soon became worse and they began to make plans to go into *hiding*. They kept their plans a *secret* from Anne and Margot.

Anne's diary gives us an insight into what it was like for Jewish people to live in Amsterdam after Hitler's army had *occupied* the Netherlands.

"Jews were required to wear a yellow star;

Jews were required to turn in their bicycles;

Jews were forbidden to use trams;

Jews were forbidden to ride in cars, even their own;

Jews were required to do their shopping between 3:00 and 5:00 p.m. . . .

Jews were forbidden to be out on the streets between 8:00 p.m. and 6:00 a.m.;

Jews were forbidden to go to theatres, cinemas or any other forms of entertainment."

Anne at school

*L*ike many teenagers today, Anne and her friends worried about **tests** at school. Many of the people in her class made bets on whether they would pass or not!

Anne was smart, but she didn't always get the top grades. She told her diary that her parents didn't worry too much about her grades, as many other parents did.

"AS LONG AS **I'm healthy** AND HAPPY and not too cheeky, THEY'RE SATISFIED."

One of Anne Frank's teachers became so frustrated with her for **talking** in class that he made her **write an essay** with the title "A Chatterbox." That didn't work, so he made her write another assignment, which she entitled "'Quack, Quack, Quack,' Said Mistress Chatterback!"

"I FINISHED MY POEM,
and it was beautiful!
IT WAS ABOUT A MOTHER DUCK
AND A FATHER SWAN WITH THREE
BABY DUCKLINGS WHO WERE
bitten to death by the father
BECAUSE THEY QUACKED TOO MUCH.
*Luckily, Keesing took the
joke the right way . . .*
SINCE THEN I'VE BEEN ALLOWED TO TALK
*and haven't been assigned
any extra homework.*"

Everything changes

On July 5, 1942, Anne's sister, Margot, received an **_order_** from the government to report to a LABOR CAMP. By this time Jewish people knew that call-up notices like this were dangerous.

LABOR CAMPS

Many Jewish people were taken to labor camps by the Nazis. They were forced to do hard physical work with hardly any food or water. Living conditions were extremely poor and people often died from starvation or disease. In addition to the labor camps there were concentration camps where Jewish people were taken to be killed.

Otto and Edith had been preparing to go into hiding for some time. Although their **preparations** were not finished, they knew that there was no time to waste – they had to get their family to *safety*.

The very next day the Frank family went into hiding. They couldn't take much with them in case anyone noticed and **reported** them to the AUTHORITIES. When they left their house for the last time, the whole family wore several **layers of clothing** so they could take as much as possible with them. But their bags of possessions were small, and they had to leave many things behind.

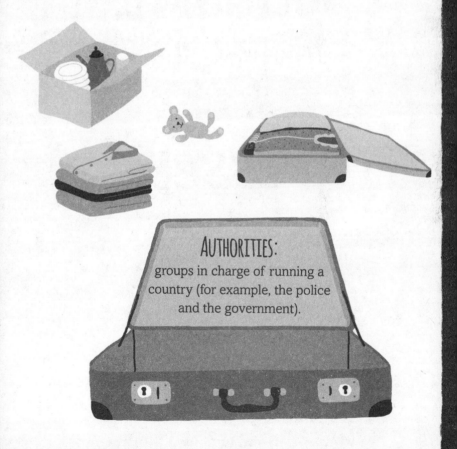

AUTHORITIES:
groups in charge of running a country (for example, the police and the government).

"MEMORIES
MEAN MORE TO ME
than
dresses."

A home behind a bookcase

The secret ANNEX that served as their hiding place was hidden in Otto Frank's office building. The building contained a warehouse, storerooms and offices. At the back, right at the top, there was a secret *set of rooms* – the Secret Annex! From the outside, no one would suspect they were there. As long as Anne's family stayed quiet and were careful, they would be safe . . .

ANNEX: a room or set of rooms added to a building after it was first built.

Soon after Anne's family moved in, a movable ***bookcase*** was built in front of the door to the Annex. It swung out so that it opened like a door. It was a clever idea that helped the people in the Annex to remain ***hidden***. No one could see the door and so no one could ask questions about where it led.

The **eight people** who hid in the Annex were: Otto, Edith, Margot and Anne Frank; Hermann, Auguste and Peter van Pels (given the code name "van Daan" by Anne in her diary) and Fritz Pfeffer (known as "Mr. Dussel" in the diary). In this book, all the people in the Annex will be called by the names that Anne used.

Did you know?

Like many teenagers, Anne liked film stars. Her father brought her collection of postcards and posters to the Annex, and Anne put them on the walls to make it seem more like home. The pictures are still on the walls today.

Layout of the Annex

They all had to share bedrooms with each other, and there was only one toilet for them all to use. They had to use a tin bath to wash.

2nd FLOOR

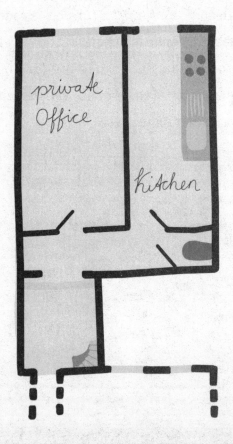

3rd FLOOR

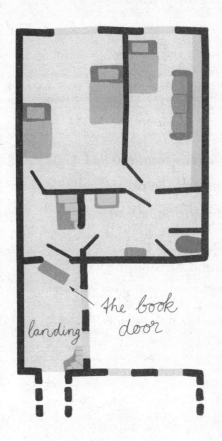

the book door

landing

4th FLOOR

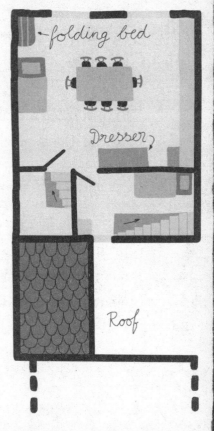

folding bed

Dresser

Roof

Anne had to share a room with Mr. Dussel, and Margot had to share with their parents. The van Daans slept in a room that was also the **kitchen**.

Life in hiding

Sometimes when the office workers had gone home for the day, Anne and the others could go into the offices below the Annex to listen to the *radio* – but they had to be very careful. Later, after the warehouse and offices had been *burgled* a couple of times, they didn't risk leaving the Annex at all and stayed upstairs at all times.

During the *two years* they lived there, none of them could *ever* go outside. The only time they got fresh air was when they had a window open at night when no one was around to see. During the day all the curtains were drawn so that there was no chance of a neighbor or passerby spotting them. It made the Annex quite dark and stuffy, especially when there was hot weather.

Food in the Annex

At first they had **plenty of food**. Otto and Edith Frank and the van Daans had taken plenty of supplies to the Annex before they moved in, so they had a good store. They also had lots of money saved up so that they could buy things on the BLACK MARKET to add to the food they got with their RATIONS.

BLACK MARKET: when things are sold illegally and secretly at high prices.

But as their time in hiding went on, food became more difficult to get. Some of their stored food went bad and prices on the black market became higher and higher.

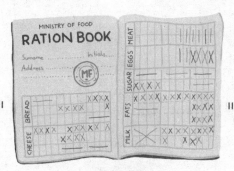

RATIONING

made sure people got a fair share of the food that was available during the war. Everyone was given a book of coupons or "rations." You were allowed to buy only certain amounts of each food (for example, cheese or meat) every week. This was to make sure there was enough to go around. People often managed to get more of the things that were rationed by buying them on the black market. It wasn't only food that was rationed but clothes and other items too.

There were also *shortages*, so many foods were not available. This meant that the people in hiding sometimes had to eat a lot of the same thing. Although this must have been hard, Anne managed to write about it in a funny way.

"FOR A LONG TIME we ate nothing but ENDIVE. ENDIVE WITH SAND, endive without sand, ENDIVE WITH MASHED POTATOES, endive and mashed potato casserole."

ENDIVE: a type of plant often eaten in salads.

It wasn't only eating lots of the same thing that was a problem. Anne and the other people in hiding sometimes had to eat food that didn't taste nice – or was *rotten*!

"*I must tell you about the* DUMPLINGS. *We make them with government-issue flour, water and yeast.* THEY'RE SO GLUEY AND TOUGH *that it feels as if you have* ROCKS IN YOUR STOMACH, *but oh well!*"

Getting along – and not getting along

With eight people living in such a small space, and unable to go out, it's not surprising that Anne wrote all about the **arguments** they had.

Anne described how tense everyone felt after one of the many fights. Sometimes at mealtimes everyone would stay silent to stop another argument from starting up!

Anne was the *youngest* of the group. She often felt as if she was criticized the most. She was very *outspoken* and not afraid to say what she thought. This got her into trouble again and again.

Anne showed herself to be many things in her diary – funny, chatty and thoughtful. She was also **very brave**. She was determined to be *cheerful* even when things were hard.

"**EVERY DAY**
I think what a
FASCINATING AND
AMUSING ADVENTURE
THIS IS!
With all that,
why should I
DESPAIR?"

The love of the outdoors

Anne told her diary that she had not given **nature** much thought before she went into hiding. However, once she was trapped indoors day and night, she began to enjoy the glimpses she had of the outside world. Anne realized how much happiness nature brought her.

She was *fascinated* and delighted by the things outside: the sky, the floating clouds, the birds flying past, a night breeze or the leaves and blossoms on the tree. The sight of these things and the feel of the wind when the window was open became precious to Anne.

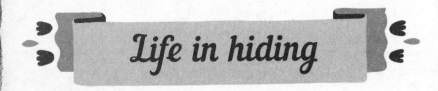

Life in hiding

*D*uring the day, while the warehouse and offices below the Annex were *busy* with workers coming and going, the people hiding upstairs had to remain *silent*.

DID YOU KNOW?

Because they had to keep quiet when people were in the office building below, they could only flush the toilet at certain times. Anne wrote in her diary that the toilet was sometimes very smelly – especially as eight people had to share it!

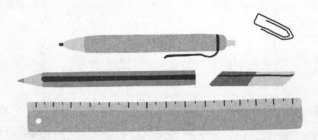

Having to be quiet for so much of the time was hard. The group had to develop their own hobbies – but they had to be quiet ones! Everyone in the Annex **studied**. Sometimes they did this by signing up for a CORRESPONDENCE COURSE. There were several people on the outside who knew about the Annex and did their best to help Anne and the others, and the lessons were mailed to one of these helpers.

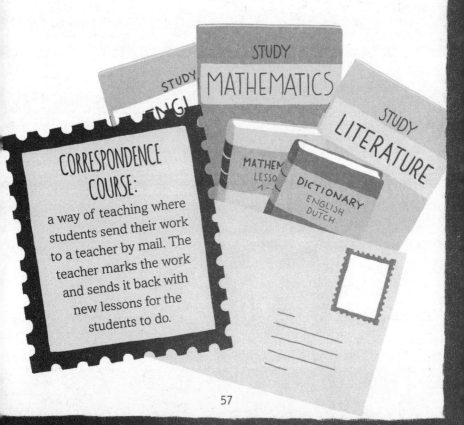

CORRESPONDENCE COURSE:
a way of teaching where students send their work to a teacher by mail. The teacher marks the work and sends it back with new lessons for the students to do.

Margot took courses in several subjects, including English, French and Latin. She also studied German literature, as well as book-keeping, geography, history and biology.

Like her sister, Anne studied many subjects. These included shorthand, geometry, history, art history and algebra – though she didn't enjoy algebra!

Everyone in the Annex was an enthusiastic **reader**. Each week one of their helpers would bring new **books** from the library. Everyone looked forward to that day.

The helpers

Everyone hiding in the Annex was very keen to know what was happening in the war. They received their **news**, both local and worldwide, from the people who came to deliver food and other supplies.

Miep Gies

Johannes Kleiman

Bep Voskuijl

Johannes Voskuijl

The helpers were Johannes Kleiman, Victor Kugler, Miep Gies, Bep Voskuijl, Jan Gies and Johannes Voskuijl, Bep's father – people who knew Anne's father from working alongside him. They were *horrified* by what was happening to the Jewish people around them and did everything they could to help their friends survive. Doing this meant *risking their own lives* and experiencing tremendous strain and hardship. Some of the helpers suffered from poor health, and the stress caused by the *responsibility* of looking after eight people on top of their own families was considerable. Anne was very conscious of how much the helpers had sacrificed and often wrote about how *grateful* she felt.

Victor Kugler

Jan Gies

People who were discovered to be helping Jewish people were arrested and sometimes even killed by the Nazis. Despite that, many people risked their lives to help others during the war. They recognized that it was vital to make a stand against Hitler.

It was very difficult to keep such an **_enormous secret_** and to bring supplies to the people in hiding, but they survived there for over two years. Without their helpers, the group would not have been able to remain undiscovered for so long.

When Anne and the others managed to listen to the radio, reports from the news channels sometimes brought bad news, sometimes good. More than anything, the people hiding wanted to know when Hitler and his army might be *defeated*. When that news came, it would mean they were *free*.

Each of them had a different idea of what they would do if the war was won and they could come out of hiding. Anne's dream was to go back to *school*, where she could have friends and be a *normal* teenage girl again.

Cats in the Annex

Anne was very fond of the two **cats** that lived in the building – they helped her stop missing Moortje, the cat she had been forced to leave behind.

The cats' names were Mouschi and Boche. Although Anne and Peter enjoyed petting the cats, they did bring some problems – including *fleas*!

"Mouschi has now proved, beyond a shadow of a doubt, THAT HAVING A CAT HAS

DISADVANTAGES

as well as advantages. THE WHOLE HOUSE IS CRAWLING WITH

FLEAS...

It's making us all

VERY JITTERY."

One day Mouschi was in the loft at the very top of the Annex, and instead of using the litter box she went on a pile of *wood shavings* over a gap in the floor. The cat's pee went down through the floorboards and into the room below!

"*I doubled up with*
LAUGHTER,
it was such a
FUNNY SIGHT."

Although living in the Annex was hard, that didn't mean it was always miserable. Despite the arguments, the group found opportunities to *laugh* and enjoy themselves too. Once, Peter van Daan was moving several heavy bags of beans up to the attic when one of the sacks split. Anne described a "hailstorm" of beans as they fell.

Did you know?
Anne really liked dressing up, and she and Peter van Daan would make everyone laugh by putting other people's clothes on.

"PETER WAS STUNNED,
but then burst into
peals of laughter
WHEN HE SAW ME STANDING
AT THE BOTTOM OF THE STAIRS,
like an island in a sea
of brown, with waves of
BEANS
lapping at my ankles."

Anne described how hard she often found life in the Annex. But she also made it clear that she understood that what lay outside was much worse. Throughout the diary Anne showed a **determination** to remain cheerful and keep busy rather than give in to despair. Even when she was aware of the most shocking events of the war, she never lost **hope** that things would one day get better. Anne always had faith that the war would end and peace would return.

Anne would also write about how **lucky** she was compared to the Jewish people who weren't in hiding. However frustrating she found being cooped up indoors with the same people day after day, she knew that it was an easier existence than many other Jewish people were enduring.

Coping with fear

During their time in the Annex the eight people hiding had to cope with many **scares**. Because people in Amsterdam were desperate for food and money, **burglaries** were common. The offices below the Annex were broken into several times. This was very dangerous because each time the building was broken into, the **police** had to be called – and every time the police looked around, there was a chance that they might discover the secret of the Annex.

The worst of the burglaries happened over a holiday weekend and led to the police returning to the building more than once. Anne and the others had to stay utterly *still and silent* to remain undiscovered. They couldn't go to the toilet downstairs and had to use wastepaper baskets. It was a terrifying two days before they knew they were safe again . . .

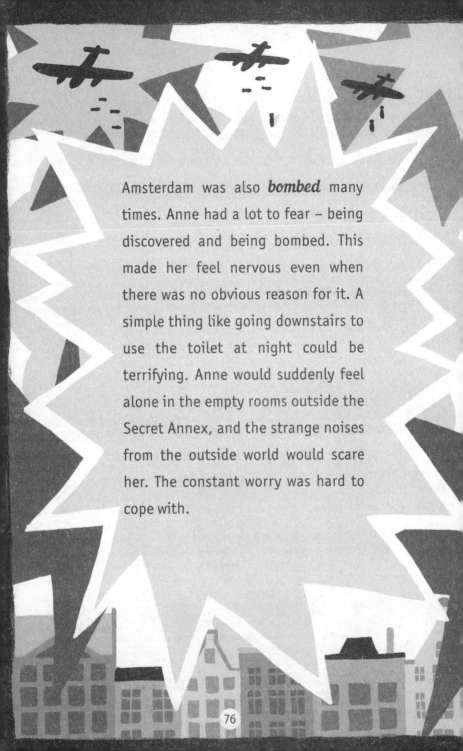

Amsterdam was also **bombed** many times. Anne had a lot to fear – being discovered and being bombed. This made her feel nervous even when there was no obvious reason for it. A simple thing like going downstairs to use the toilet at night could be terrifying. Anne would suddenly feel alone in the empty rooms outside the Secret Annex, and the strange noises from the outside world would scare her. The constant worry was hard to cope with.

Anne came up with a funny way of dealing with the fear brought on by the noise of gunfire.

When she heard guns she would begin running up and down the stairs.

She wrote that the noise and the grazes she got from falling over would take her mind off the fear.

Anne's *diary* was something that helped her deal with the fears she and the others experienced while they were in the Annex. Anne found that writing was a *comfort* and helped her cope with the sound of the bombs, the burglaries and the fear of being discovered.

"WHEN I WRITE
I can shake off
ALL MY CARES.
My sorrow
disappears,
MY SPIRITS ARE
REVIVED!"

Anne was *thirteen* years old when she went into hiding. She changed a great deal during the two years she was in the Annex.

09.25.1942

08.05.1944

On March 28, 1944, a radio BROADCAST asked people to **keep records** of the German occupation of the Netherlands, including diaries. After hearing this Anne decided that she would *rewrite* her diary so that it could be considered for publication after the war. From the time of the broadcast until she left the Annex, Anne worked on a new story based on what she had written in her diary. She kept writing the diary too. In only seventy-six days she managed to fill nearly **two hundred** sheets of paper!

BROADCAST:
a program that you listen to on the radio.

"MY GREATEST WISH

is to be a

JOURNALIST,

and later on,

A FAMOUS

WRITER."

DID YOU KNOW?

Anne wrote other things as well as
her diary. While she was in hiding she
wrote lots of short stories and kept a
collection of special quotes.

Found out

*I*n the early summer of 1944 news from the outside world brought hope to Anne and the others. The Allies were making progress in their fight against the Axis powers, and the end of the war seemed to be in sight. On June 6, 1944, (known as D-Day), the Allies invaded *Normandy* – victory for the Allies seemed to be on its way. Anne wrote that the news of the invasion had given them all *fresh courage* and made them feel stronger. Anne even dreamed of being able to go back to school and lead a normal life.

However, although the **end of the war** was close, the luck of those in hiding had run out. On the morning of August 4, a Nazi officer and members of the security police arrived and made their way to the Secret Annex. Someone had told the authorities about the people in hiding. No one has ever found out who **betrayed** them.

They were arrested and taken to prison before being sent on to different camps.

After being held in prison Anne, Margot and their mother were taken to the Auschwitz-Birkenau concentration camp in Poland.

At first all three were kept in the same area of the camp, where they were made to work. They had to carry rocks or other heavy loads even when they became weak from hunger.

Then, in October 1944, the two sisters were moved to Bergen-Belsen prison camp in Germany. Their mother never knew where they had been taken, and eventually in January 1945, overwhelmed by illness and distress, she died.

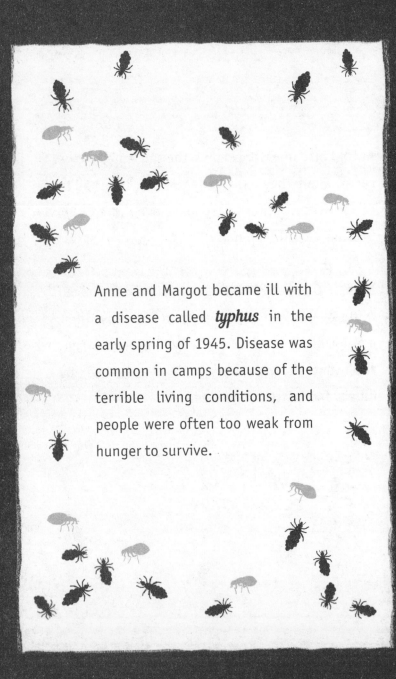

Anne and Margot became ill with a disease called *typhus* in the early spring of 1945. Disease was common in camps because of the terrible living conditions, and people were often too weak from hunger to survive.

Margot finally died of the disease, and Anne followed just a few days later. Their official date of death was given as March 31, but it now seems likely that they died in *February*.

Of those who had been in hiding, some were killed at the camps and some died from hunger and exhaustion. Only one of the group from the Secret Annex survived the war: Anne's father, Otto.

Otto Frank had remained at Auschwitz-Birkenau camp and was **released** on January 27, 1945, when it was liberated at the end of the war. He didn't discover that his daughters had died until he returned home when the war was over.

When Otto Frank arrived in Amsterdam, one of the helpers gave him Anne's diary. She had rescued it after the arrest and kept it hidden, hoping she would one day be able to return it to Anne. Reading her words, Otto discovered how *thoughtful* and *inspiring* Anne had been.

He was astonished by the *quality* of Anne's writing, and after showing parts of it to friends and family he realized what an *important* document it was. The diary described the *reality* of living through the war as a Jewish person and the fears experienced by those who tried to hide from the Nazis. It was also a study of a lively and enormously likeable girl in extraordinary circumstances growing up.

The mixture of these two things meant that people everywhere found Anne's story *gripping*.

The discovery of Anne's diary was a comfort to Otto because it gave him a *purpose*. He spent the rest of his life trying to make Anne's dream of being a famous writer come true, spreading her messages of hope for human rights and understanding. And he succeeded!

Anne's dreams come true

Today Anne Frank is one of the most famous writers of the twentieth century.

Otto Frank found a small publishing company that was willing to publish the diary. The *first edition* was published in 1947. The 3,000 copies sold out quickly and another edition appeared just six months later. At first other countries were not keen to publish the diary, but in 1952 a woman called Judith Jones, who worked for the publisher Doubleday, pulled the diary out of a rejection pile and decided that she had to publish it. Since then the book has been translated into over seventy languages and has sold more than *25 million copies*!

The diary was also turned into a *stage play* in 1955. Although Otto Frank worked endlessly to spread the word about his daughter's writing, he found it too hard to watch the play and did not attend performances of the first production.

In 1960 the Secret Annex and the office building were opened as a museum. Ever since, thousands of people have visited the rooms where the eight hid for over two years and where Anne wrote her extraordinary diary. It is still possible to see the posters of film stars on the walls of the room where she slept.

Anne's story goes on

As well as the many editions of the diary that have been published across the world, Anne's writing has been explored in other ways. In addition to the stage play there have been films, television programs, a radio play and songs inspired by her story.

Anne's diary continues to help us understand what it was like for a Jewish person to live in a country occupied by the Nazis. People who read it are inspired to ensure that the **terrible events** of the Second World War do not happen again. Anne's extraordinary story makes us want a world where children like Anne can grow up and live to see their dreams come true.

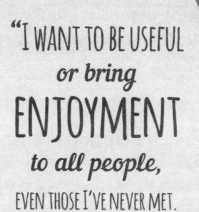

1929

Anne Frank is born in Frankfurt am Main, Germany, on June 12.

1933

Adolf Hitler comes to power as the leader of the Nazi party. Anne Frank's family decide to leave Germany after Jewish people are mistreated.

1934

Anne's family move to Amsterdam.

1942

On July 5, Margot Frank receives a letter telling her to report to a German work camp.

The Franks, the van Pels (van Daans) and Fritz Pfeffer (Mr. Dussel) go into hiding.

1939

The Second World War begins on September 1, when Germany invades Poland.

Margot Frank
Ph.:-L l d .].- 48
1155 Amsterdam

1940

Hitler's army invades the Netherlands and the Dutch army surrenders. The Nazis occupy the country and anti-Jewish rules are put in place. Otto Frank and his wife begin preparations to go into hiding.

Jood

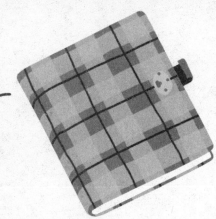

1942-1944

For the two years that Anne Frank is in hiding, she keeps a record of her experiences in a diary.

1944

On August 4, the authorities arrive and arrest everyone in the Annex and two of their helpers. Anne and the others are taken away to camps with thousands of other Jewish people.

1945

Margot and Anne become ill with a disease called typhus. They die within a few days of each other, most likely in February, and not long before the camp is liberated from the Germans.
On May 8, Germany surrenders and the Second World War ends.

1952

Anne's diary is published in the English language for the first time.

1947

Otto Frank has Anne's diary published.

1960

On May 3, the Annex and office building are opened as a museum. Hundreds of thousands of people have since come to visit the place where Anne lived and told her story to the pages of her diary.

Some things to think about

Anne's diary tells us about some of the things that Jewish people were not allowed to do after the Germans came to power. Can you imagine what it would be like if you had to live by different rules than everyone else? How would you feel if you were suddenly prevented from going to the houses of your friends, or from visiting places with them? What would it be like to be barred from using any kind of transportation and to have to walk everywhere?

If you had to leave your home suddenly, what would you pack? Would you take your most treasured possessions or more practical things, like food and clothes?

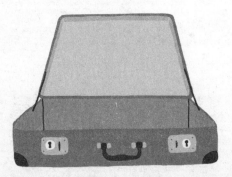

"*In the face of melancholy . . .*
MY ADVICE IS:
'*Go outside, to the country,*
ENJOY THE SUN
AND ALL NATURE HAS TO OFFER.
Go outside and try
to recapture
THE HAPPINESS
WITHIN YOURSELF . . .
and in everything around
you and be happy.'"

What do you think we can learn from Anne and her approach to life? Do you think she was right not to complain about her situation and to try to remain strong and cheerful?

Can you imagine never being able to go outside? What would you miss most? The feel of a breeze? The sound of wind in the trees?

What would you do to pass the time if you couldn't make any noise? Can you imagine a world without any modern technology – no television or tablets or phones to watch or listen to?

Index

Auschwitz-Birkenau camp 86–87, 90

Bergen-Belsen camp 87

Dussel, Mr. 41, 43

Frank, Anne
    at Auschwitz-Birkenau camp 86–87
    at Bergen-Belsen camp 87–89
    at school 30–33
    birth and childhood 12–16
    cats 66–69
    cheerfulness 52–53, 72–53, 105–106
    coping with fear 74–79
    diary 2, 7–10, 23–26, 78, 81–82, 90–99
    food 46–50
    found out 4, 84–86
    getting along with others 51–52, 70–71
    and helpers 61
    illness and death 88–89
    life in Amsterdam 20–29
    life in hiding 1–4, 34–45, 51–52, 56–58, 64–65, 70–71, 80
    love of the outdoors 56–57, 105–106
    timeline 100–103

Frank, Edith 20, 36, 41, 43, 87

Frank, Margot 12, 20, 34, 41, 43, 58
    at Auschwitz-Birkenau camp 86–87
    at Bergen-Belsen camp 87–89
    illness and death 88–89

Frank, Otto 20, 61, 89, 90
    and Anne's diary 6–7, 90–96
    in hiding 36, 41, 43

Gies, Jan 61

Gies, Miep 61

Hitler, Adolf 14–15

Jewish people 12, 15, 19, 73
    helpers 60–63
    labor camps 34–35
    restrictions on 28–29

Jones, Judith 94

Kleiman, Johannes 61

Kugler, Victor 61

Nazis 15, 18, 35, 62, 85

Pfeffer, Fritz see Dussel, Mr.

Second World War 18–19, 27, 84

Secret Annex 2, 39–44, 97
    burglaries 74–75
    cats 66–69
    discovery 85
    food 46–50
    helpers 60–63
    life in hiding 44–45, 51–52, 56–58, 64, 70–71

van Dann (van Pels), Auguste 41, 43

van Dann (van Pels), Hermann 41, 43

van Dann (van Pels), Peter 41, 43, 66, 70–71

Voskuijl, Bep 61

Voskuijl, Johannes 61

Quote Sources

Direct quotes throughout are from *Anne Frank: The Diary of a Young Girl,* The Definitive Edition edited by Otto H. Frank and Mirjam Pressler (Penguin Books, 2012)

Have you read about all of these extraordinary people?